1950–2012

# The Brits Who Built The Modern World

1750–1950

## Empire Builders

Today – Tomorrow

## A Global Era

RIBA
Architecture.com

# Contents

# Introduction

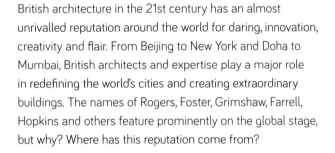

British architecture in the 21st century has an almost unrivalled reputation around the world for daring, innovation, creativity and flair. From Beijing to New York and Doha to Mumbai, British architects and expertise play a major role in redefining the world's cities and creating extraordinary buildings. The names of Rogers, Foster, Grimshaw, Farrell, Hopkins and others feature prominently on the global stage, but why? Where has this reputation come from?

In the first half of the 20th century, while there was a revolutionary movement in European and American architecture based on the use of new materials and technologies, the dominant style of building continued to be influenced by classical and vernacular traditions. As an imperial power, Britain continued to take these styles to all corners of its Empire as it had done in the 19th century. However, this approach to building was out of step with a changing world.

How, then, did a nation relinquishing its imperial role adapt to this new world order and become such a key player in shaping international architecture and design? What did British architects do to capture the attention of so many?

Using the RIBA's unique collections, this book tells a global story of British architecture between 1750 and the present day. Inspired by the BBC series *The Brits Who Built The Modern World*, and following the narrative of three exhibitions mounted by the RIBA in 2014, it explores what and where the British built and the reasons behind architecture's dramatic transformation in the post-war years. Through the work of a definitive generation of architects and other key players, it charts the projects and influences that put British architecture on the world map.

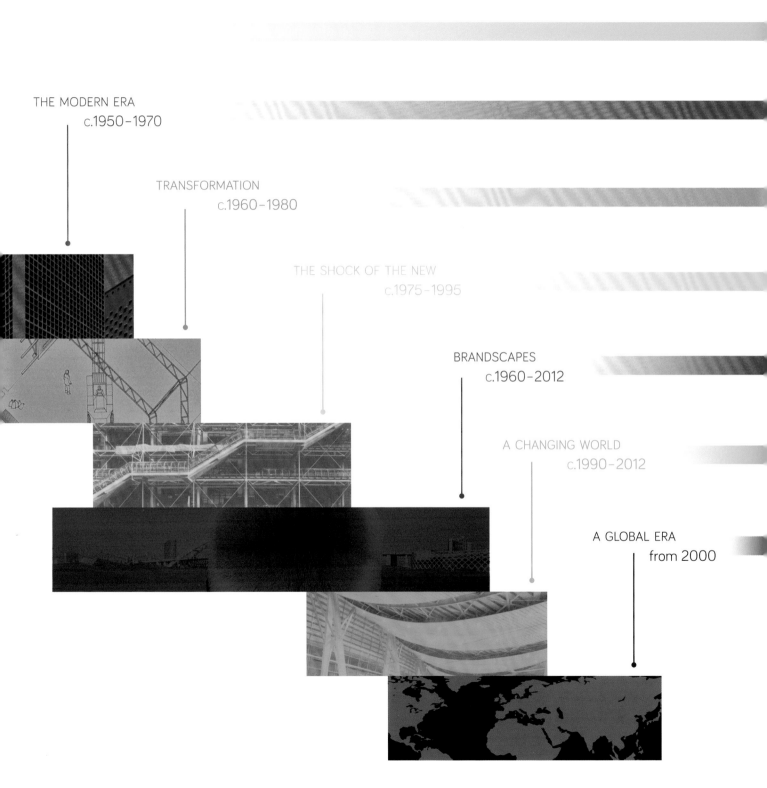

THE MODERN ERA
c.1950–1970

TRANSFORMATION
c.1960–1980

THE SHOCK OF THE NEW
c.1975–1995

BRANDSCAPES
c.1960–2012

A CHANGING WORLD
c.1990–2012

A GLOBAL ERA
from 2000

# GLOBAL VIEWS

Five architects on working
internationally

# A story of Asia

BY TERRY FARRELL

After finishing my Harkness-funded master's degree at the University of
Pennsylvania, I was awarded RIBA scholarships to study in Japan. I arrived just
a few weeks before the 1964 Tokyo Olympics and was driven around the new
buildings by Fumihiko Maki in his old Mercedes. I took photos, one of which (the
new Olympic pool by Kenzo Tange) appeared on the front cover of the first colour
edition of the *RIBA Journal* just after my return.

I then flew via Kyoto to Hong Kong to be shown around by a former Newcastle
classmate, Cecil Chao. All of these experiences heightened my early, and then
lifelong, awareness of the powerful growth and energy of China and the Far East.
I returned to Asia briefly in 1980 to open an office and again, permanently,
in 1991.

I have been fortunate to have had many Chinese and Asian personal friends
(and, in time, to marry my wife Mei Xin) and to have had a continuous connection
with the region all of my life. The extraordinary story of the Far East over the
past 50 years has been a privilege to be close to, particularly as this century will
belong to Asia.

# The Hongkong Bank

## BY NORMAN FOSTER

The bank was in many ways the first global building; it was assembled from a range of elements that came from many diverse places – from America, from Europe and from Japan. I think the contrast of technology is interesting. The bamboo scaffolding, for example. I don't think it would be possible to realise this building without that indigenous bamboo scaffolding – which erupts everywhere – any more than it would without the cranes by which it erects itself. At the peak of the construction programme we had 4,500 people living and working on the site. It has to be said that attitudes to safety were, at that time, somewhat different to what we were used to – and this produced some incredible photo opportunities. At one point our slide library had a whole section of images of the Hongkong Bank entitled 'Danglers'!

When we went out to be interviewed for the Hongkong and Shanghai Bank project, we stayed on in Hong Kong, after our competitors had left, to discover how the banking hall worked at the ground level. It was only after that research that we were able to demonstrate the feasibility of putting the banking hall up in the air so that there is this transparent showcase, with a glass underbelly, that creates a public space at ground level. That space also created a new social focus in the city. Whenever I go to Hong Kong I always take photographs there. At the weekend it is the liveliest picnic spot in the city. Significantly, it also allowed the bank to develop the site at a better than 18 to 1 plot ratio, which is an extraordinarily efficient use of land. At that time experienced developers in Hong Kong could not achieve better than a 14 to 1 ratio. We were outsiders but we managed to better that at our first attempt.

# Responding to climate

BY NICK GRIMSHAW

One of the critical factors about working abroad is the influence of climate. We made this a key issue when we were working on the competition for Expo '92 in Seville – the hottest city in Europe. It did not make sense to use traditional heavyweight materials such as brick and stone to keep the building cool, as the structure was only in place for about six months.

Nevertheless, we were determined not to make the building an air-conditioned box like so many of the other pavilions. We shielded all the walls from the direct impact of the sun and used power from solar cells on the roof to pump water to the top of the east façade, where it ran down the face of the building creating substantial cooling. Out of the 105 national pavilions at the Expo '92, the British Pavilion used the least energy.

At the other end of the temperature scale, we realised when designing Pulkovo Airport that there was a strong desire by our clients to avoid the normally disruptive effects of snow that they had to endure during the winter. We inverted the roof so that the snow could not slide off, while also using it as insulation to help prevent heat loss.

No matter where we are working in the world, I feel it is vital to respond to the climate. One should never 'import' a solution and try to make it fit the climate. The climate itself should control the situation and the building should respond.

# Happenstance

## BY MICHAEL HOPKINS

Working abroad for us has always been through 'happenstance' rather than carefully planned intent.

After working on an abortive project for Mitsubishi in the City of London, they invited us to enter a small, and paid for, competition for their prime site in Maranouchi, across the square from Tokyo Station, along the axis to the Imperial Palace. Carrying out the project from London and working with Mitsubishi's engineers, we produced a building that is popular in Tokyo, and successful for both Mitsubishi and ourselves.

Separately and three years later, with a small daughter office in Tokyo, Simon Fraser, our partner in Dubai, won another invited competition to design a quite different, but similarly large multi-use building in the Theatre district, fronting Hibiya Park for Mitsui. Enabling construction began in autumn 2013.

Lectures sometimes set off a whole chain of projects. In 2000 I was asked to talk at the American University in Dubai. With family about to be posted there, I accepted. My talk was attended by Joseph Tabet, who saw the natural ventilation systems we were working on in the UK. He asked us to design a group of 60 houses, making the best use of the breezes that naturally occur along the Gulf coast. Designed in London, this led to a branch office in Dubai run by Simon Fraser and a series of successful projects over the past decade. Joseph Tabet remains a friend and mentor.

Likewise, a visit to the office in London by the environmentalist Stephen Kellert, followed by his invitation to lecture at Yale, led to our university projects on the American East Coast. First was the School of Environmental Studies at Yale, followed by the Frick Chemistry building at Princeton and two residential colleges at Rice, Texas. It was an enjoyable and successful run, brought to a crawl by the recession.

# The Pompidou Centre

## BY RICHARD ROGERS

Renzo Piano, Su Rogers and I formed a practice principally because it's more fun to be three unemployed architects than one. For the Pompidou Centre, Ted Happold of Arup approached us to take part in the competition. Su and I were against it, while Renzo and Ted thought it was a good idea. When it came to the final decision, Su was out of the office, as one of our children was sick, and I therefore lost the vote.

The Pompidou Centre presented many complex hurdles, not least the competition submission. Marco Goldschmeid took a large roll of drawings to the post office a few minutes before the deadline, only to be told by the assistant that the package was too big for the UK post. Marco borrowed a pair of blunt scissors and cut down our drawings on the rather grimy post office floor.

After we won, we were viciously attacked in the courts and the press over the next six years and only had two positive reviews, both in the *New York Times*. Luckily, we were naïve enough that we didn't understand it was more or less impossible to build a centre of that size in a country that had a rule that foreign architects were not allowed to design large public buildings.

One day, I was standing across from the site in the rain and a little old French lady offered to share her umbrella with me. She asked me what I thought of the building and I stupidly told her I was the architect. She promptly hit me over the head with her umbrella. C'est la vie!

# New worlds

Sainsbury Centre for the
Visual Arts, University
of East Anglia, Norwich,
1978. Foster Associates.

# Hugh Pearman
EDITOR, RIBA JOURNAL

Sometime in the mid-1970s, a friend and I, driving south from our north-eastern university, decided to make a detour to the University of East Anglia. We shared an entirely amateur liking for modern architecture, the more concrete-and-glass the better. The new National Theatre in London was about to open, and we liked that. But we knew of these earlier buildings by the same architect, Denys Lasdun: a new-wave university, much bolder than our own, where the students lived in space-age ziggurats set in a grassy landscape. We got there in my friend's aircooled primrose-yellow Citroen GS, which looked exactly right in these surroundings, and duly marvelled at the ziggurats. And then, strolling around, we found something else.

It was still being built, but its metallic shell was in place. It was an enormous, long hangar of a building, with glass ends and a frame of tubular steel spars, entirely unlike the Lasdun mother ship to which it was tethered at an angle. We peered in at one end and speculated as to what it was for. Not teaching, not living, not a library or students' union, yet in a university: it must be some kind of sports hall, we concluded as we drove off. This was my first, unconscious, exposure to a building by Norman Foster. It was, I later discovered, the Sainsbury Centre – a combined art gallery, student centre and arts faculty. Somewhat altered and much extended by Foster over the years, and always nurtured by the philanthropic Sainsbury family, who donated their art collection to it, it is now a Grade II* listed building.

That moment marked the changing of the guard in British architecture. Lasdun's heavyweight approach had evolved from his 1930s youth, working with concrete-modernist pioneers Tecton. Foster's arose from a new sensibility: he had studied in America with another now world-famous architect, Richard Rogers, and later

Buckminster Fuller, 1968. Pictured with exploratory models of the lightweight geodesic structures that would shape his career and influence many around the world.

worked with him. The two men had found conventional building techniques to be a messy, wet, almost Victorian business: why couldn't buildings be more like cars or ships or the construction toy Meccano, assembled from dry, prefabricated components? This was not a new idea: as early as the Festival of Britain in 1951, architects were predicting a science-fiction future. But it took a while to arrive.

Along with many architects of the time, Foster had sat at the feet of visionary American engineer-inventor Richard Buckminster Fuller, an early environmentalist. It was Fuller, whose opinion was sought on the Sainsbury Centre design, who asked Foster what was to become a famous, oft-quoted question: 'How much does your building weigh?' The future, it seemed, was lightweight and clip-on. Over in Paris, Rogers was about to complete the Pompidou Centre with fellow architect Renzo Piano, which looked like nothing that had ever been built before and was an absolute revelation. And so I found myself entering a career of writing about architecture, just as what came to be known as 'High Tech' was rising to international prominence.

When we talk about *The Brits Who Built The Modern World*
it is this generation of architects –including Nicholas
Grimshaw, Michael and Patty Hopkins and Terry Farrell –
that springs most readily to mind. Where older generations
of architects, some of them included in this book, had had
the Empire to provide a ready-made market, they did not
– with the notable exception of booming Hong Kong. All
the more remarkable, then, that they were able to export
this approach to other nations and turn it into a global, and
globally recognised, commodity. Not simultaneously – Rogers
was the first to internationalise, the Hopkinses the last. By
the 1980s, other styles and other names were coming into
play, with the likes of cool modernist David Chipperfield and
his stylistic opposite, the highly theatrical 'narrative architect'
Nigel Coates, working in Japan. They had to: in a stagnant
UK economy, there was no work for them back home. This
echoed the post-industrial British way in general: as old-
fashioned manufacturing industry shrank, service industries,
including design, flourished. British architecture itself had
undergone a self-induced crisis in 1974, when growing
public dissatisfaction with post-war redevelopments and
the perceived aloofness of the profession led to the start of
a fundamental, even agonised, reappraisal. This took many
forms – one was a rediscovery of 'vernacular' architecture,
reconnecting modernism with traditionalism, which got a
mixed reception. But the High Tech new guard, who ripped
up preconceived ideas and started from scratch, were hailed
as heroes. Their shiny, futuristic buildings photographed
beautifully. Picture editors around the world loved them.

High Tech had the ability to surf over the retro decade of the
1980s, when much British architecture seemed to consist of
what evolutionary scientists would call 'hopeful monsters'

Kowloon Station, Hong Kong, 1998–2002. Farrells.
The station building itself represented the 'tip of
an iceberg', being the first step in the creation of
an entirely new piece of city.

in the form of ever more outré Post Modern buildings. Most of these exercises were doomed to early extinction, though some proved exportable, notably in the hands of James Stirling (an influential teacher of the new generation, as well as a great architect in his own right) and Terry Farrell, who enthusiastically embraced Post Modernism. Stirling became big in Germany and America, as did Foster, Grimshaw and Chipperfield. Farrell followed Foster to Hong Kong, and eventually to Beijing. More restrained modernism reasserted itself in the 1990s.

By the start of the 21st century it was stylistic open house and a remarkable new talent was making her mark on the international stage. Zaha Hadid's extraordinarily original buildings took a while to gain acceptance but, once they did, she found herself in demand globally. The year 2014 finds British architects building around the world at an unprecedented level, working especially in the new markets of Asia and the Far East. The futuristic journey begun by British architects in the Skylon and Dome of Discovery in 1951 has finally achieved escape velocity.

Terminal 4, Barajas Airport, Madrid, Spain, 2006. Rogers Stirk Harbour + Partners.

From the middle of the 18th century until the dissolution of the British Empire after the Second World War, British architects and builders found many opportunities to work abroad. Architecture first followed trade routes and then, as trading posts often became springboards for territorial acquisitions, there was a growing requirement to erect buildings for government, religion, housing, education and pleasure. It was common in the older colonies with more temperate climates for architects to emigrate, whilst in the tropics, and in India in particular, careers were shorter and, if they survived, architects retired back to the mother country. British dominance of international trade meant that architecture became a commodity exportable to other countries outside the Empire. From the 1840s, architects participated in international competitions and a hundred years earlier, they were already accepting commissions from expatriates and Anglophiles.

After the founding of the Royal Institute of British Architects (RIBA) in 1834, many architects sent back drawings and photographs of their work for its collections. For architects who had emigrated, membership of the Institute was prized as an important testament of their status and abilities and they were proud to use the initials FRIBA and ARIBA to indicate that they were Fellows or Associates. These overseas memberships, as well as the gifts of drawings and photographs, helped to bind the British profession internationally in a way that no foreign architectural institutes could match.

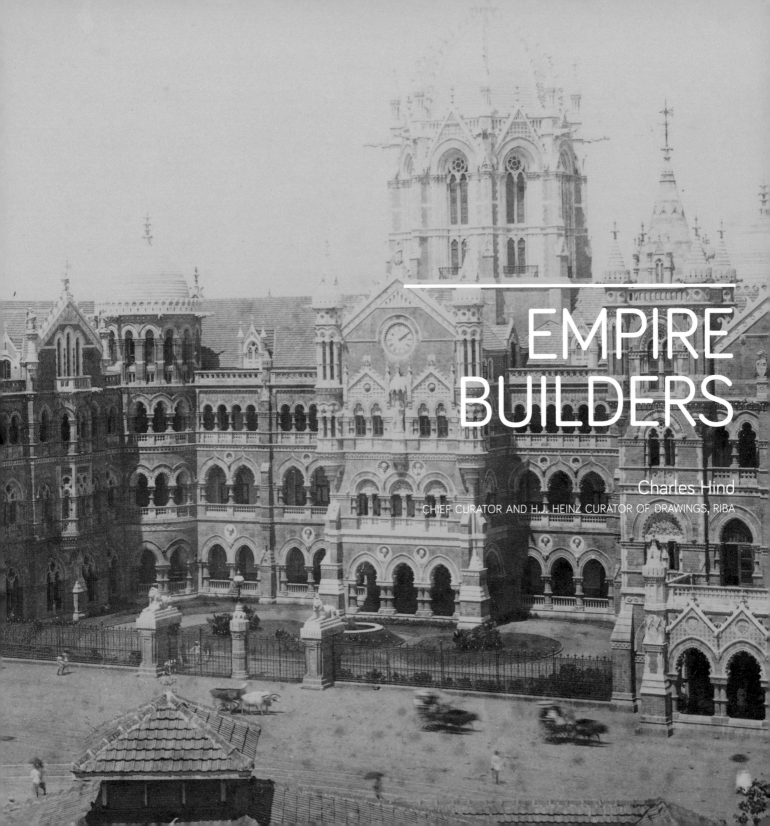

# EMPIRE BUILDERS

Charles Hind

CHIEF CURATOR AND H.J. HEINZ CURATOR OF DRAWINGS, RIBA

## TRADE AND COMMERCE

Britain's international standing was based on her power
as a trading nation. The earliest buildings connected with
commercial activity appeared in the American colonies in the
early 17th century and in India 50 years later. Commercial
buildings, however, have tended to be ephemeral and early
examples are rare because they were often replaced as social
and economic needs changed, or they fell victim to war, fire
and hurricanes. But the buildings that facilitated trade and
communication, such as railway stations and post offices,
were often built on such a monumental scale that many
survive today.

## GOVERNMENT

The earliest colonial structures associated with government
were designed to be practical rather than to create grand
effects but, by the early 19th century, there was a growing
appetite for more ambitious buildings. In 1805, Lord Valentia,
the Governor-General of India, replied to criticisms of the
expense of the new Government House in Calcutta with,
'I wish India to be ruled from a palace, not a counting house,
with the ideas of a Prince, not those of a retail dealer in
muslin and indigo'. The new Government House was built
on a huge scale and to a design that was derived from a
great English country house, Kedleston Hall, Derbyshire.
Its symbolism was potent and numerous Indian princes
subsequently commissioned British architects (or, more often,
military engineers) to build classical palaces that were Anglo-
Palladian in style.

Frederick William Stevens, FRIBA (1848–
1900). Victoria Railway Terminus, Bombay,
India. Albumen print photograph by Arthur
Gill, c. 1885.

Frank Lewis Worthington Simon FRIBA (1862–1933) and
Henry Boddington ARIBA (1881–1965). The model for the
Manitoba Legislative Building, Winnipeg, Manitoba, Canada.
Gelatine-silver photograph by Foote and James, 1920.

## EDUCATION

As Britain's empire grew, opportunities to build large government buildings increased, from courts of justice and town halls to new parliaments. Such buildings in Australia, Canada and South Africa were expressions of the growing confidence of the self-governing Dominions. By the early 20th century, even regional assemblies were demanding imposing homes. The Manitoba Legislative Building was as large as some European parliaments. Only in New Delhi was there both the funds and the will to build a completely new imperial capital. It was completed barely a decade before India achieved independence.

From the early 19th century, British and colonial governments increased expenditure on education when it was realised that an educated population was more economically productive. The design of educational buildings overseas often reflected British models, such as the older public schools and universities. Educating 'subject peoples' to university level had the unintended effect of creating effective opposition to British rule. This proved fatal to the hopes of those who, as late as the 1950s, still believed that the decolonisation of Africa was generations away. The architectural legacies of these education policies often remain impressive and still function, even in very different political environments.

Cyril Arthur Farey FRIBA (1888–1954) and Graham Dawbarn FRIBA (1893–1976). Perspective of a design for the Administration Block, Raffles College, Singapore, c. 1922.

# HOME FROM HOME

Successive waves of emigrants from Britain during the 19th century expected all the amenities of British life in their new environments. Often surprisingly quickly, the disorder of early pioneer settlements evolved into planned towns and cities. Architects were commissioned to build museums, hospitals, theatres, cemeteries and that very British institution, the Club. Standards were expected to be high. The new opera house in Valletta, Malta, was designed by the same architect, E. M. Barry, who had just rebuilt the Royal Opera House, Covent Garden.

# RELIGION

The British built churches all over the world in places where they traded or had diplomatic representation. They were always built where the British had established a degree of political control. Until the mid-19th century, the most frequently used classical model was James Gibbs's London church of St Martin-in-the-Fields (completed in 1726). It inspired churches from Charleston in South Carolina to Penang in modern Malaysia. One of the earliest versions built in India had a lower tower than the original because it was necessary to omit a storey in order to reduce the weight that was bearing down on soft ground. The Gothic Revival style took a firm hold from the 1850s. In general, British church architects building abroad adhered far more closely to the prevailing taste in Britain than they did when designing any other building type. Only rarely did British architects build religious buildings other than churches.

James Barnet, FRIBA (1827–1904). Perspective view of a design for Haslam's Creek (later Rookwood) Mortuary Station, Sydney, Australia, 1865.

Lieutenant James Agg (c. 1758–1828). St John's Church, Calcutta, India. Aquatint after J. B. Fraser, published in 1826.

## ADAPTING THE BRITISH STYLE

Reflecting a desire to keep up with fashion and from feelings of homesickness, house builders tended to follow styles that were popular in Britain. These ranged from Palladianism in the early American colonies to Art Deco and modernism later in India, Africa and elsewhere. Architects abroad used pattern books, and later on building and architectural journals, to keep up to date with the styles of the mother country. However, the planning of houses tended to be adaptable to local requirements. Apart from churches, the bungalow became the most widespread building type in the British Empire and beyond.

## RESPONSES TO CLIMATE

British architects and builders varied in their reactions to the many widely diverse climates in which they built. In India, what became the ubiquitous bungalow was first developed by adapting traditional Bengal houses with their verandas and high-pitched roofs. The type soon found its way into every part of the world and a variant with a flat roof was used in hot, dry climates. West European Gothic and classical styles proved adaptable to local conditions and building techniques. It was unusual to transplant wholly English-style buildings abroad unless the climate was similar to Britain's or the client was especially homesick. However, some interesting hybrids emerged. The Arts and Crafts architect C. F. A. Voysey, who was known for his English vernacular style houses, built a winter home for an English doctor in the Egyptian desert that looked as though it had strayed from Surrey, although with a flat roof.

Sir Ernest George RA, PRIBA (1839–1922) of Sir Ernest George & Yeates. Perspective view of a design of a bungalow, Nairobi, Kenya, 1918.

Charles Francis Annesley Voysey FRIBA (1857–1941). Designs for a house for Dr Leigh Canney, Aswan, Egypt, 1905.

## ANGLOPHILES AND EXPATRIATES

During the 19th and early 20th centuries, contemporary British domestic architecture enjoyed an international reputation. Anglophile foreigners commissioned British architects, often for reasons of prestige. Though he never saw it, the Regency architect Edward Blore designed a particularly successful hybrid Muslim/Tudor Gothic house overlooking the Black Sea for a Russian aristocrat, Prince Mikhail Worontsov, who had spent much of his childhood in London. Towards the end of the period, increasing numbers of British clients living abroad also began to commission houses from British architects.

Edward Blore (1787–1879). Perspective of a design for the Aloupka Palace, Yalta, Crimea, Ukraine, begun 1830.

Oliver Hill, FRIBA (1887–1968). Perspective of a design for a house in Tsinan (now Jinan), China, begun 1922, for Peter and Helena Wright.

## IMPERIAL MEMORIALS

Many British men and women who went abroad never returned home and the world is littered with monuments to British dead. They commemorate civilians who died abroad while working, or those who had vainly gone for the sake of their health. Many, both civilian and military, died in the service of the British Empire. The millions who died in the First and Second World Wars are commemorated by the largest and best-maintained memorials. One of the most moving is the Menin Gate at Ypres, which bears the names of 54,896 soldiers who have no known graves.

Sir Reginald Blomfield, RA, PRIBA (1856–1943). Perspective of a design for the Menin Gate Memorial to the Missing, Ypres, Belgium, c. 1923.

## PROBLEMS AND FRUSTRATIONS

Building abroad did present challenges. Many of the 18th- and early 19th-century buildings in India were designed by military engineers whose working lives, in a difficult climate, were often short. Many died young or, like Major Charles Mant, went mad from overwork. Problems of a different sort could arise when trying to control a project from England. William Burges won the competition to design the Crimea Memorial Church in Constantinople in 1856 on a site donated by the Sultan of Turkey. But as the site kept moving and the budget shrank, in 1863 he resigned the commission in frustration.

## THE POST-WAR EFFORT

The Second World War led to a collapse in overseas work. The dissolution of the Empire from 1947 and the growing self-confidence of the Dominions and their home-grown architects were balanced by the huge amount of work architects had at home, building for the welfare state and rebuilding the bombed cities of Britain. Some architects maintained active practices in former African colonies, the Commonwealth and in the Middle East, but the 1950s and 1960s were a hiatus marked by the wrapping up and winding down of an old era and the dawn of a new one.

William Burges, FRIBA (1827–1881). Perspective drawing of the proposed Crimea Memorial Church, Constantinople (now Istanbul), Turkey, 1856.

During the early post-war years the world was changing dramatically. Old certainties and even older empires were disappearing. With the independence of its former colonies and America's status firmly established as the world's superpower, Britain's old imperial narrative was in conflict with a new age. Expectations and attitudes were shifting and the world was in the grip of a massive drive to modernise.

Fuelled by a consumer boom, goods and services were evermore widely exchanged and the advent of the jet aircraft meant that once-remote places could be reached in hours instead of days or weeks. For architecture, it was the dawn of a new and progressive age.

Heavily influenced by early modern masters such as Le Corbusier and by ideas from Scandinavia and mainland Europe, British architects adopted modernism to construct a positive national story. For other nations, architecture served to demonstrate a world view and a position as an international contender.

During this time the horizons of British architects changed. For those at home there was a country to rebuild, while for those working outside the UK there were few guarantees. Architects were now part of an emerging competitive global marketplace. Working in far-off lands, they extended a modern style to new audiences.

# THE MODERN ERA

Mike Althorpe
PUBLIC PROGRAMMES, RIBA

# A new narrative at home

After the war, a new and convincing British story was essential to win over hearts and minds. In 1951, the Government-produced Festival of Britain offered ration-weary Britons a glimpse of a better future through new architecture, design and daring feats of engineering. It had a profound influence, kick-starting a process of state-led reconstruction and renewal across the UK.

The Skylon at the Festival of Britain, London, 1951. Powell & Moya. This structure became a beacon for a brighter future. With its lightweight materials and naked structural expression, it was a sophisticated marriage of engineering and architecture. Perceived by many at the time as a novelty, it would have a longstanding influence.

Alton West Estate, Roehampton, London, 1955–1959. London County Council Architects Department. The design of this large council estate was typical of many that went up in the UK at the time. Following European models, flats and maisonettes were arranged in towers or horizontal blocks and set in large communal open spaces. Concrete was used extensively. The structures became an essential part of the UK's new landscape.

# Getting out there

British architects abroad in the post-war years catered for a world that was skilling up and speeding up. Education provision was a key first step in transforming economies, with many new universities and colleges established to cater for new nations and growing populations. At the same time, an entirely new landscape of airports, offices, hotels and conference centres emerged in response to the demands and expectations of heads of state and an increasingly global business traveller.

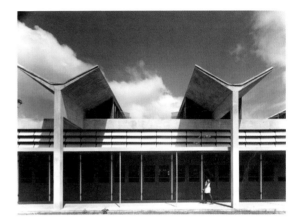

College of Technology, Kumasi, Ghana, 1956. James Cubitt & Partners. Founded in 1952, the college was granted university status in 1961, becoming the Kwame Nkrumah University of Science and Technology of Ghana.

Library at the University College, Ibadan, Nigeria, 1955. Fry, Drew & Partners. Many young British architects first worked abroad in the former British Empire, renamed the 'Commonwealth'. Buildings were completed in a style that – inspired by the climate – quickly became known as 'Tropical Modernism.'

'It's a small world by Speedbird' BOAC poster, c. 1950. F. H. K. Henrion. Bigger, faster and safer aircraft ushered in a post-war boom in the numbers of people flying and the places they could go. International business and the spread of ideas flourished and a new global language in operations, expectations and diplomacy was established.

British Petroleum head office, Lagos, Nigeria, 1961. Fry, Drew & Partners. New commercial buildings embraced a modern world architectural language. A brise-soleil sun shading system is shown here extending across the façade to keep the spaces inside cool – a technique used extensively in an age before air-conditioning became commonplace.

View of the new Abadan Airport, Iran, 1960. Brian Colquhoun & Partners. Beginning life as a military airstrip in World War II, the airport, like many in the region, was rebuilt for new commercial services to meet the demands of emerging international business concerns. In this case that derived from nearby oil fields.

National Bank of Dubai headquarters building, Dubai, 1971. John R. Harris & Partners. The prestigious building is seen here overlooking the historic Dubai Creek and harbour and shows the juxtaposition of old and new trading in the city at a period of immense change.

The main entrance of the King Faisal Conference Centre, Riyadh, Saudi Arabia, 1973. Trevor Dannatt & Partners. The outcome of a limited international competition of 1966 and directly approved by King Faisal, the centre was part of a strategy to bring new activity to the capital city of Riyadh at a time of massive expansion.

Straining away from the ideas and conventions of early 20th-century modern masters, the younger generation was increasingly dissatisfied with the conventions of post-war architecture, both at home and abroad. Starting in schools of architecture on both sides of the Atlantic, and inspired by a world beyond British influence, they felt that architecture had essentially failed to embrace the possibilities of things that society everywhere else was taking for granted. Materials such as plastics, aluminium, glass and super-strong steel were now common. Yet concrete, brick and plaster continued to dominate building design.

Despite the declaration by Prime Minister Harold Wilson in the 1960s that the UK was 'burning with the white heat of technology', building design still followed the lessons in shape and form established at least three decades previously. There was a crisis of confidence in architecture. It seemed that the great adventure in modernism that had swept the globe was losing its momentum.

Responding to this new mood and, by the 1970s, to an increasingly challenging economic climate, an interconnected group of young architects ushered in a new era of experimentation in the UK that they would, in time, take out to the wider world.

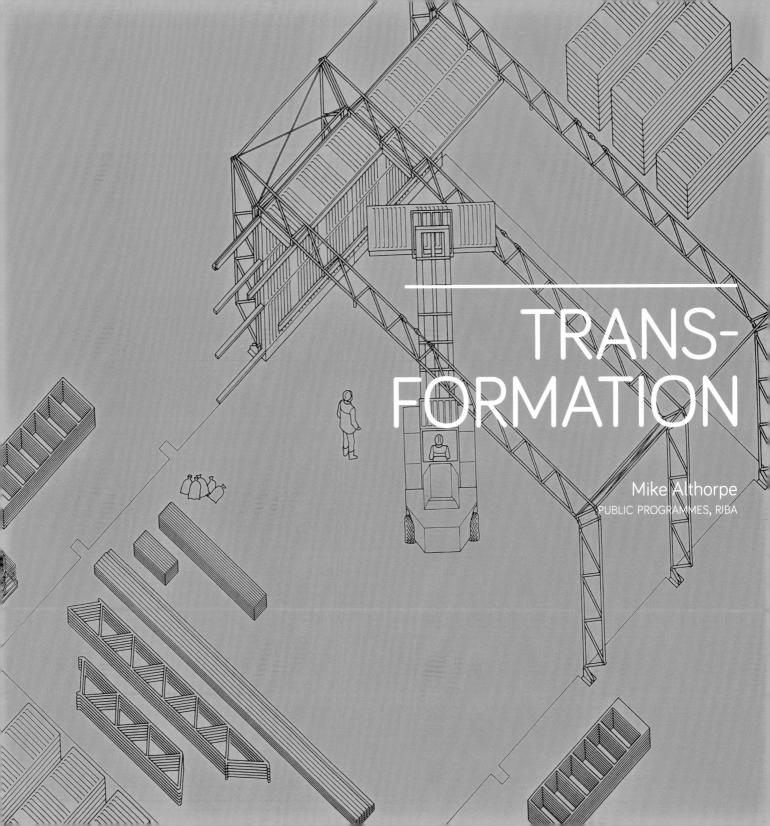

# TRANS-
# FORMATION

Mike Althorpe
PUBLIC PROGRAMMES, RIBA

# America, America!

In the 1950s and 1960s, the United States of America came to dominate nearly all aspects of popular culture. For the younger generation in the UK, images of its great cities, its consumer products, music and art left them spellbound. It was a place of potency, energy and modernity. Its universities attracted architectural talent from across the world and formed an essential part of what would become a transatlantic exchange of ideas.

'Fly to USA by B.O.A.C' advert, c. 1950. Frank Wootton. America and its vertiginous cityscapes increasingly caught the attention of a younger generation of architects and proved seductive to many. The country epitomised both the glamour and progress of a new world.

The Mercury-Atlas 8 rocket carrying astronaut Walter M. Schirra Jr lifts off from Cape Canaveral, Florida, USA. October 3, 1962. The dawning of the space age sent imaginations running wild and America was at the forefront of this 'new frontier.' Inspired by its energy and raw technical aesthetic, architects and designers in all fields speculated on how it could change the way we lived.

# New faces

Born within a decade of each other, the generation that came to reshape British architecture came from a range of backgrounds and architectural experiences. Informed by travel and liberated by the creative environments of prominent schools of architecture in the USA and the UK, they shared many common concerns, heroes and influences. As friends, collaborators, colleagues and partners they completed their first projects in response to a new social and economic era.

Nicholas Grimshaw, c.1968. Born in 1939, Grimshaw graduated from the Architectural Association in 1965. He set up practice with Terry Farrell in the late 1960s and established Nicholas Grimshaw and Partners Ltd in 1980, now known as Grimshaw Architects LLP.

Richard & Su Rogers, early 1960s. Born in 1933, Richard Rogers met Su at Yale University in 1962 where both met Norman Foster. They established the practice Team 4 together in 1963. Richard and Su went into partnership in 1967 before Richard established Piano + Rogers with Renzo Piano in 1971. In 1977 the Richard Rogers Partnership was created, known as Rogers Stirk Harbour + Partners since 2007.

Norman Foster, 1971. Born in 1935, after Foster graduated from Manchester University School of Architecture and City Planning in 1961 he went to Yale University, USA where he gained a Master's Degree in Architecture. In 1963 he co-founded the practice Team 4 with Richard Rogers and in 1967 established Foster Associates, now known as Foster + Partners.

Michael Hopkins, late 1970s. Born in 1935, Hopkins graduated from the Architectural Association in 1964, having previously worked for architects Frederick Gibberd and Basil Spence. In 1969 he went into partnership with Norman Foster and in 1976 established Hopkins Architects with wife Patricia Hopkins.

Patricia Hopkins, 1985. Born in 1942, Patricia graduated from the Architectural Association in 1968. She co-founded Hopkins Architects in 1976.

Terry Farrell, early 1980s. Born in 1938, Farrell graduated from the University of Newcastle in 1961 and gained a masters from the University of Pennsylvania, USA, in 1962. He set up practice with Nicholas Grimshaw in the 1960s, and in 1980 formed Terry Farrell & Partners, today known as Farrells.

# Pop goes architecture

Inspired by the possibilities of the consumer age and new methods of production, students and architects began speculating on a radical architecture for the future that could be 'life enhancing'. Music and fashion at this time had undergone a revolution, why should there not be a similar revolution in the way buildings and entire cities were created? By adopting engineering techniques and utilising products developed elsewhere, architects were able to make a leap into thinking about totally new spaces in which to work, to experience culture, to socialise and to play.

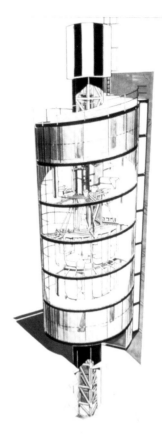

Service Tower of the Students' Hostel, Bayswater, London, 1967. Farrell Grimshaw Partnership. An exercise in 'pragmatic radicalism', this innovative structure, by a very young architectural partnership, housed a vertical stack of bathroom 'pods' with a helical ramp surrounding them. The tower meant that the fabric of the adjacent historic building could be left intact – it was a solution that seemed perfectly in step with changing times.

'The Climatron', Blackpool, final-year student design thesis, 1961. Terry Farrell. Influenced by Buckminster Fuller, this scheme proposed a vast indoor holiday island raised on legs and connected to the base of Blackpool Tower. Its multipurpose spaces anticipated future building types and an economy based on recreation.

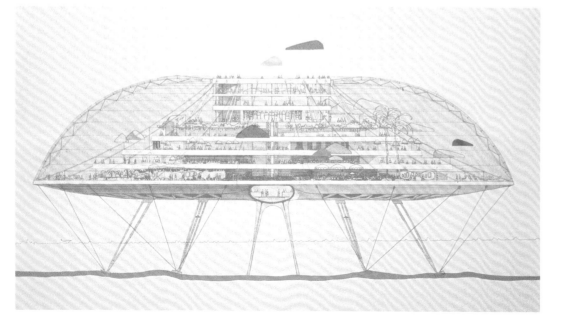

**FACING**
United States Pavilion, Expo '67, Montreal, 1967. R. Buckminster Fuller & Sadao. This massive 'geodesic dome' was the high point of many years of experimentation in efficient building types by its creator. Fuller's 'more with less' approach and focus on structural lightness proved hugely influencial for many British architects.

# Systems thinking

Prefabricated components for buildings were in widespread use during the 19th century for creating spectacular glasshouses, train sheds, bridges and temporary structures. However, the equivalent approach in the post-war years had gained a reputation for utility and meanness, with many doubting whether it was capable of producing great architecture. Using new materials with economy, architects demonstrated that it was possible to create functional buildings with flair and elegance. Techniques and principles developed originally for industry and one-off houses were applied at a steadily increasing scale, achieving even greater drama and hinting at the shape of things to come.

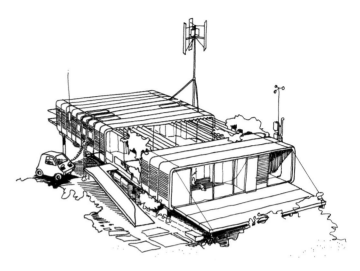

Concept drawing for the Zip Up House, 1968. Richard & Su Rogers. This conceptual design was based on creating a building from standardised components, such as refrigerator panels, to make an energy-efficient home.

Electronic components factory for Reliance Controls Limited, Swindon, Wiltshire, 1967. Team 4. Built quickly and cheaply using prefabricated components, this building broke new ground by placing all workers and management functions under one roof. Its light partition walls meant it could be expanded rapidly. It was one of the first in a new breed of commercial buildings, well suited to the explosive growth of something later referred to as the business park.

Eames House, Pacific Palisades, Los Angeles, 1950. Charles & Ray Eames. The work of many modern American designers inspired an interest in new materials, structural simplicity and industrial techniques. By employing such methods construction could be speedier, cheaper and readily reproduced.

Interior view of the Hopkins House, London, 1976. Michael and Patty Hopkins. Construction techniques developed for larger commercial buildings and factories were used in this family home. A grid of unadorned lattice trusses and columns supports floors and ceilings and the walls are made of sheets of insulated metal.

B&B Italia Offices, Como, Italy, 1973. Piano + Rogers. Described as a 'small scale dress rehearsal' for the much larger Pompidou Centre in Paris, this building established a new structural and aesthetic approach, with bold colour used to accentuate external elements. The partnership of Rogers and the Italian architect Renzo Piano was to prove critical in taking a new architecture to new parts of the world.

Factory for Herman Miller Furniture Company, Bath, 1977. Farrell and Grimshaw Partnership. Built for the company that made famous many design innovations, such as the Eames Chair, this building employed a lightweight cladding design to create a modern and innovative exterior. In 2013 it was Grade II listed.

In the late 1970s and throughout the 1980s a strange
and unexpected thing happened to British architecture – it
became the most talked about in the world. At a time of
massive economic upheaval in the UK, a series of projects
were completed at home and abroad that caught the world's
attention, transforming the reputations of their creators in
the process.

Established international figures were joined by a new
generation of architects whose distinctive approach caused
shock waves. It was a period of profound change. Reaction
against the anonymous tower blocks of an earlier era was
pushing architecture in a variety of directions. Advocates of
a radical modern architecture were matched by those who
favoured a return to traditional forms.

Two style labels entered the lexicon and came to define the era:
'High Tech' and 'Post Modern'. Working in America, Europe and
the Far East, British architects carved out a new, richer identity
for modern architecture. One style in particular – High Tech –
was to become the defining international style of the late
20th century.

After decades of looking outwards and importing the most
exciting ideas, British architects reached a point where they, in
turn, became innovators, exporting a confident new architecture
abroad. The 'Brits' had come of age.

# THE
# SHOCK
# OF THE
# NEW

Mike Althorpe
PUBLIC PROGRAMMES, RIBA

# High drama

By the late 1970s, High Tech was a firmly established name for an architectural style, sometimes referred to as 'structural expressionism' or the 'industrial style'. The completion of two seminal international projects in Paris and Hong Kong catapulted it into the world's consciousness. High Tech architecture was characterised by the use of high-performance materials, the expression of undisguised structural elements and the celebration of everyday technical and functional components. It was an approach that saw air ducts, ventilation and service cores, as much as steel trusses and cross-braces, become part of the articulation and visual drama of a building.

Pompidou Centre (Centre National d'Art and de Culture Georges-Pompidou), Paris, 1977. Piano + Rogers. Conceived in the aftermath of the 1968 Paris riots, the competition for this enormous contemporary arts centre attracted 681 entries from around the world. The winning scheme proclaimed 'a live centre of information, entertainment and culture'. It was a radical departure from anything seen before and launched the global career of its British and Italian creators. Its giant steel frame supports five enormous floors of flexible exhibition space.

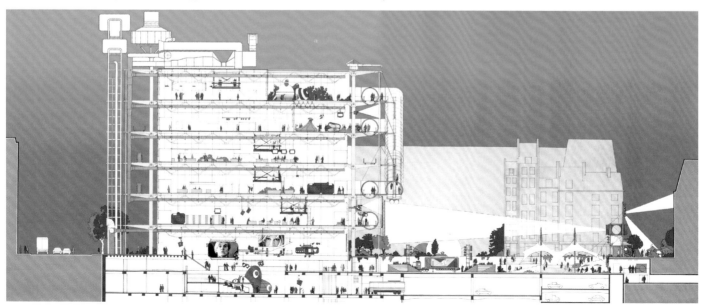

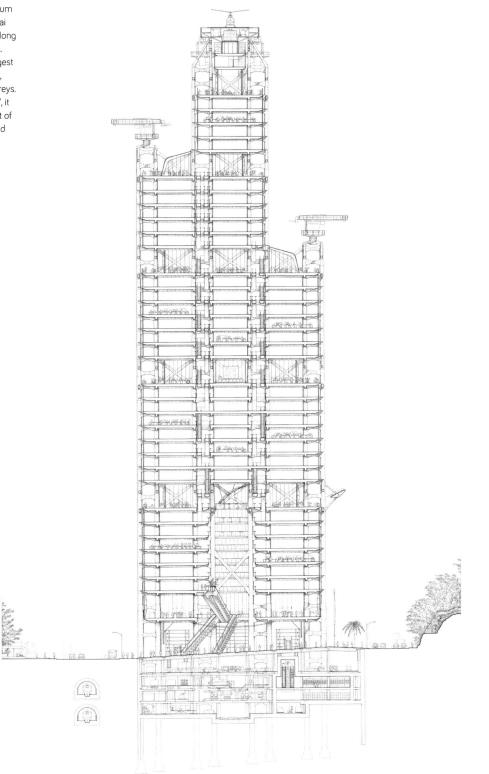

Cross section through the atrium of the Hongkong and Shanghai (HSBC) Bank Headquarters, Hong Kong, 1985. Foster Associates. This vast building was the largest by the practice who, until then, had not built above seven storeys. 'Created without compromise', it represented a huge statement of confidence for the practice and forged a global reputation.

Hongkong and Shanghai Bank Headquarters. Hong Kong, 1985. Foster Associates. The building is articulated in stages and clusters of activity. Structural masts linked to large trusses support the floors and dramatically animate the building's façades.

PA Technology
Laboratories
(Patscenter), Princeton,
USA, 1985. Richard
Rogers Partnership.
This building extended
Rogers' colourful
language of structural
steelwork and was one
of British High Tech's
first ventures outside
Europe. Its bold form
made a dramatic mark
on the landscape. North
American Universities
would prove to be great
patrons of a new
British architecture.

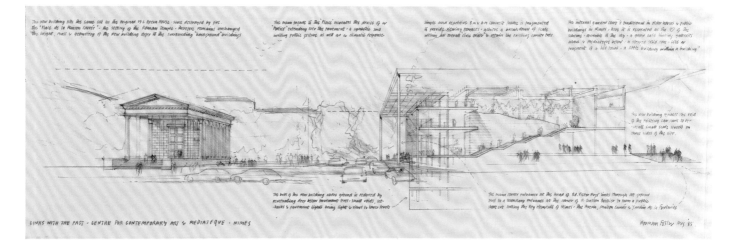

Sketch section of the Carré d'Art, Nimes, France, 1993. Norman Foster. The contextual relationship between the new arts centre and the Maison Carrée – a Roman temple built in 5 AD – is explored. While the building approached its historical setting with caution, its design avoided pastiche. It was 'of its age', extending a contemporary tradition. The debate over the intervention of contemporary architecture into heritage sites continues today in many parts of the world.

Ignus Factory and Headquarters, Cologne, Germany, 1992. Nicholas Grimshaw & Partners. Built to a challenging brief that required both a landmark and a set of manufacturing spaces where 'anything could happen anywhere,' the building uses giant masts and a network of cables both as a means of support and as visual 'excitement'. The legacy of the 1951 Skylon can be seen in its central masts.

# High Tech at home

Stretching, suspending and climbing new heights, architects were often able to court the world's attention without leaving the UK. New landmarks at home cemented a reputation for daring and innovation overseas, while extending what was steadily becoming known as a new British approach.

Schlumberger Research Centre, Cambridge, (Phase 1), 1985. Michael Hopkins & Partners. This flambuoyant building marked a breakthrough in its use of materials. Its billowing fabric roof structures are in Teflon-coated fibreglass – then the first large-scale use in the UK. They are suspended by a 'cat's cradle of cables' that distribute weight like a suspension bridge. Through many other schemes, tension structures of this kind were to become part of the visual language of the practice.

Lloyd's Building, London, 1986. Richard Rogers Partnership. Commissioned soon after the Pompidou Centre, this building attracted global attention and divided opinion. Set within London's financial heart, it was a radical gesture. An almost gothic arrangement of ducts, lifts and stairwells surrounds a large central atrium. In 2011, it was listed Grade I – the youngest building to achieve such a status.

# A global style debate

By the 1980s, architecture abroad came to reflect the many style debates in the UK. The world was shifting, and architectural shape and form responded in a variety of ways to circumstances and context. In these years, a modernist look continued in many places, but it was 'Post Modernism' that captured the mood of the times, crossing over into graphic design, film and fashion. Its looser approach was comfortable with historical references and jumped between traditional and modern technologies. But 'PoMo', as it was called, was a short-lived style.

Neue Staatsgalerie, Stuttgart, Germany, 1977–1984. James Stirling, Michael Wilford & Associates. With its curving landscape of masonry and steelwork, the project transformed the international standing of its architect. Already a well-known figure in the UK, Stirling had built extensively in the 1960s. With this scheme he made a radical stylistic departure, stimulating an appetite for a new Post Modern look.

European Investment Bank, Kirchberg, Luxembourg, 1981. Denys Lasdun. With its strong horizontal massing and distinct landscape of terraces, this building extended Lasdun's language of modernism abroad for the first time. Conceived many years before, it opened during a wide-ranging stylistic debate that dominated the 1980s. It remains one of his most significant projects.

The Peak Tower, Hong Kong, 1991–1995. Farrells. Clad in vast sheets of aluminium, the building was the first international project by its architect Terry Farrell. The winning entry of a limited international competition, it was intended as a new landmark for the city, standing at one of its highest points. Its vast form with projecting eaves demonstrated great structural daring, while introducing a contemporary take on traditional Chinese architecture. The project enabled the practice to expand, opening its first overseas office that year – kick-starting a long relationship with the Far East.

Embankment Place, London, 1990. Terry Farrell & Partners. With its large arching form evoking a long vanished train shed of the 1860s, the office scheme was conceived as a small piece of city linking up spaces and different uses around and above London's Charing Cross Station. It was one of several Post Modern landmarks designed by the practice in the UK that established an international reputation.

'Reputation, reputation, reputation.' Businesses in any sector rely on a sound reputation for delivering goods, services and experiences. The same can be said of nations and cities. The image or 'brand identity' of a place helps us to reach decisions, supports choices and, importantly, creates desire.

Embassies, Expo buildings and Olympic stadia are examples of official generators and supporters of national brand. They offer an opportunity for states to tell others what they represent and where their expertise lies. Abroad, when buildings of any kind by British architects are well received and create excitement, 'Brand UK' and a host of interconnected industries get a boost.

During the 1990s and 2000s, cities across the world spent vast amounts of money reinventing themselves. As old industries disappeared in some places, and in others wars and regimes came to an end, the urge to attract international tourism and new business forced change at an accelerated rate. For architects, the new aspirations of civic leaders throughout the world became an essential motivator. New landmarks and world class facilities became potent symbols of change and national dynamism.

# BRAND-SCAPES

## Mike Althorpe
PUBLIC PROGRAMMES, RIBA

# Brand UK

Architecture is an essential part of the UK's identity at home and abroad. The poster here is one of several produced by the UK Government for overseas audiences, and uses work by British architects to sell both an image of this country and the creative and technical services that enabled their construction.

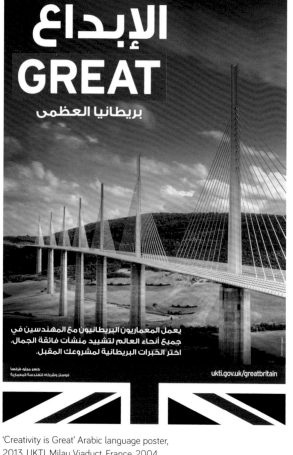

'Creativity is Great' Arabic language poster, 2013. UKTI. Milau Viaduct, France, 2004. Fosters + Partners.

# City states

In the 1990s and 2000s, achieving what became known as the 'Bilbao Effect' was the global urban doctrine of the age. Following that city's example, there was a boom in the creation of new avant-garde cultural venues and visitor infrastructure, such as airports and urban mass transit systems. The character of architecture shifted dramatically. In pursuit of the 'icon' or 'signature' look, buildings were pushed, pulled, stretched and suspended in an ever-increasing number of ways.

Guggenheim Museum, Bilbao, Spain, 1997. Frank Gehry. Hailed by American architect Philip Johnson as 'the greatest building of our time,' it transformed attitudes towards cultural buildings and ushered in the 'icon' as a means to relaunch cities all over the world. Its vast landscape of glass and titanium steel spawned a generation of dramatic structures redefining architectural style and pushing engineering to its limits. British architects learnt from its example.

Bilbao Metro, Spain, 1988–1995
and 1997–2004. Foster Associates.
The new metro system was the first
step in the strategic reinvention of
the Basque city through architecture
and infrastructure. The distinct
curving entrances announcing the
system at street level – locally
referred to as 'Fosteritos' – have
become an essential part of the
urban fabric of the city.

Interior view of the MAXXI National
Museum of XXI Century Arts, Rome,
Italy, 2009. Zaha Hadid Architects. This
building was unlike anything seen in
Rome before and an extraordinary leap
of faith for a city keen to re-present itself.
Hadid's avant-garde structures have
created one of the most high profile
architectural brands in the world today.

# National taste

Over the course of the past 60 years from 1951 to the Shanghai Expo of 2010, official buildings have played a vital role in containing and defining national image. From communicating diplomacy and democratic openness, to technological prowess and scientific enlightenment, architecture has been, and continues to be, a symbol for a whole range of values.

British Embassy, Berlin, Germany, 2000. Michael Wilford & Partners. The new German capital witnessed a massive boom in the construction of diplomatic buildings, as nation states relocated from the former West Germany. Intense competition for both location and prominence triggered an international style battle.

Design for the British Pavilion, Expo '67, Montreal, Canada, 1965. Basil Spence. Spence's design took the form of a massive white pavilion made up of two cantilevered halls and a monumental 200ft tower set out on a stepped concourse. Spence himself described it as 'craggy, tough and uncompromising'.

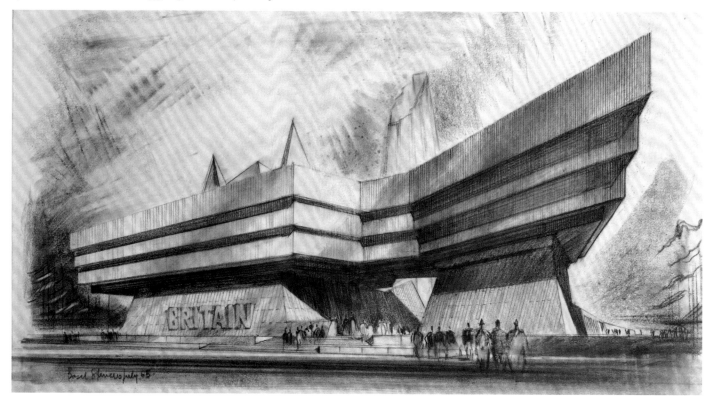

Night view of the British Pavilion, Expo '92, Seville, Spain, 1992. Nicholas Grimshaw & Partners. Characterised by its structural clarity, the external finishes of this landmark temporary building varied in response to climate. Solar panels on the roof provided energy to drive pumps to a façade that supported a water wall and another wall formed of a stack of water-filled freight containers.

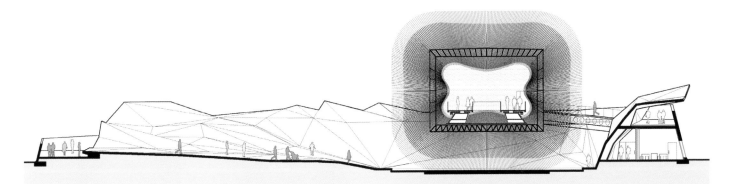

Detail of Seed Cathedral, UK Pavilion for the Shanghai World Expo 2010, China. Heatherwick Studio. In contrast to many others, the pavilion was a simple structural statement both outside and in. Instead of showy audio visual displays it showcased 250,000 seeds – encased in the tips of acrylic rods – a symbol of human nutrition and medicine. The pavilion itself occupied just one-fifth of the site with the rest providing space to relax and enjoy.

During the 1990s the world became more integrated. Increased financial liquidity, shifting consumer habits and the Internet all put people in touch with a wider world of information.

Driven by soaring populations and rapid industrialisation, new cities in China, India and the Middle East developed at a phenomenal rate. In less than a decade they grew to a scale that had taken London and Paris many hundreds of years to achieve. The pace of change defined a new age of ambition.

To meet the demands of expanding economies, many more British architects took their business to the international arena. New technologies and engineering techniques brought ever more dazzling structures to new audiences. Operating all over the world, architecture, like many other industries, became increasingly multinational and multidisciplinary, offering services that included the planning of entire cities.

When the global boom turned to slump in 2008, this brought the reminder that, like all endeavours, architecture could not act in isolation. As older European and North American economies became laden with debt, the importance of emerging economies, notably in the Far East, became apparent. The schism in world affairs marked a dramatic shift in the balance of world power and the sources of new business.

# A
# CHANGING
# WORLD

Mike Althorpe
PUBLIC PROGRAMMES, RIBA

# Extending a language

As economies modernised and new ones emerged, architecture embraced the opportunities this presented. British architects extended a language of openness and transparency in places from which they had traditionally imported ideas. In the years that followed, style badges were dropped, but the DNA of their structural origins was everywhere to be seen. At the same time, often still pushing engineering boundaries, a new architecture of 'solidity and poise' emerged in the very different work of architects such as Zaha Hadid and David Chipperfield.

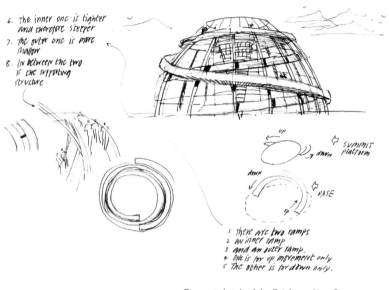

6. The inner one is tighter and therefore steeper
7. The outer one is more shallow
8. In between the two is the supporting structure.

up
down
summit platform

down
up
base

1 There are two ramps
2 An inner ramp
3 and an outer ramp.
4 One is for up movement only
5 The other is for down only.

Concept sketch of the Reichstag New German Parliament, Berlin, Germany, 1992–1999. Norman Foster. Prompted by the client's preference for the cupola rather than a 'lighthouse' as first proposed, this scheme explores the idea of spiralling ramps as a means to move through the structure.

Kroon Hall, Yale University, New Haven, USA, 2009. Hopkins Architects. Repairing a neglected piece of the historic campus, this building became a new focal point. It exported to the United States a home-grown expertise in creating a breed of 'sensitive buildings' that could feature traditional materials, but also be extremely high-performing and show stopping.

Reichstag, New German Parliament, Berlin, 1999. Foster + Partners. Such was the significance of this project when the competition was launched in 1992 many people, including its own architect Norman Foster, doubted whether a 'foreign' British architect could win. Its completion marked a huge milestone in the history of Germany and it became an instant symbol of a united democratic nation. Berlin became a significant place for British architects at this time.

Bordeaux Law Courts, Bordeaux, France, 1998. Richard Rogers Partnership. The result of an international competition in 1992, this building aimed to create a positive perception of the French judicial system through a feeling of openness and transparency. The design concept involved 'liberating' the court rooms – shown here as individual pods – from the 'box' and the creation of public space.

Southern Cross Station, Melbourne, Australia, 2006. Grimshaw Architects. Part of a major rethink of the role of the station at the heart of the city, the design focus is the 'dune-like' roof that extends to cover an entire urban block. Its undulating shape was developed in response to the hot external climate and the internal need for diesel fume extraction and cooling via natural ventilation.

Hoenheim-Nord Terminus and car park, Strasbourg, France, 2001. Zaha Hadid Architects. The rapid expansion of Hadid's practice in the 2000s saw her go from building almost nothing to employing 400 people worldwide in 2013. This project was one of her earliest abroad and often labelled as 'deconstructivist' – its form deriving from an interest in 'breaking visual rules' and pushing engineering to its limits.

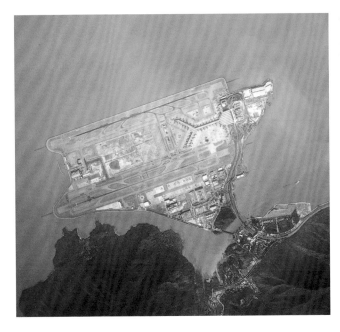

Aerial view of Hong Kong International Airport, Chek Lap Kok, Hong Kong, 1998. Foster + Partners. Among the most ambitious construction projects of modern times, the land on which this huge airport stands was once a mountainous island. In a major reclamation programme, its 100m peak was reduced to 7m and the island expanded to four times its original area. By the close of the 20th century airports would leap in scale and transform entire cities.

Interior view of Barajas Airport, Madrid, Spain, 2006. Rogers Stirk Harbour + Partners. This major project remains one of the largest the practice has undertaken. It enabled Madrid at a stroke to become a major European air traffic hub. The core consists of a series of parallel blocks, unified by an overarching roof structure capable of expansion as the airport grows. Colour is used to enliven the spaces and aid navigation.

Ciutat de la Justicia (Law Courts), Barcelona, Spain, 2009. David Chipperfield Architects. Working in many parts of the world, Chipperfield took a very different approach from those around him. Often employing traditional materials, such as stone, in large format, his buildings are often said to belong to a 'modernist tradition' and suggest permanence and solidity.

# More than architecture

The space for architecture in the 2000s was determined by a series of international events that had been set in motion years earlier. Chinese economic reforms in 1976, the fall of the Berlin Wall in 1989, and the collapse of the Soviet Union in 1992 all proved critical for the world – and the buildings – that emerged in the late 20th and early 21st centuries. In sharp contrast, the Iranian revolution of 1979 also proved pivotal in determining where British architects would not work.

Sketch of completed Tehran Bus Terminal, Tehran, Iran, 1979. Building Design Partnership (BDP). Completed just prior to the Iranian Revolution, and conceived at a time when Iran was a booming marketplace for British firms, this large building contained facilities for up to 850 long distance bus movements and 50,000 passengers a day. By the late 1970s, BDP had a large international portfolio with projects in Saudi Arabia, Egypt, the Philippines and Portugal.

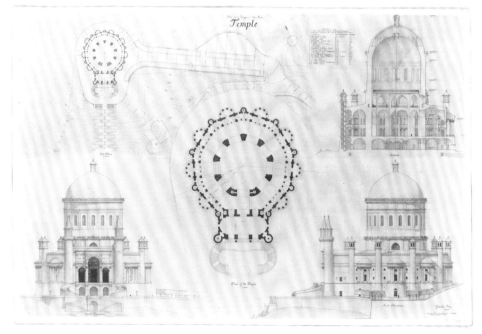

Site presentation of the unbuilt Bahá'í Temple, Tehran, Iran, 1975. Raymond Erith/Quinlan Terry. This great temple would have been one of the largest religious buildings in the Arab world. The project was abandoned when the site and the property of the religious client were seized after the Iranian revolution. The *Financial Times* in 1979 put the combined value of business losses of overseas investors in Iran at £38 billion. The loss of Iran as a marketplace in the Middle East helped spur on the development of other states nearby.

View of Dubai, United Arab Emirates, 2009.
Leaping up in scale and height, Dubai in the 2000s
threw off its old image to become one of the
fastest growing cities in the world. It marketed itself
vigorously as a 'wonder of the world' and grew to
become not just a space for business, but somewhere
to holiday, to consume culture and to live. It became
synonymous with a new age of ambition.

Gate Village, Dubai International Finance Center, Dubai, United Arab
Emirates, 2008. Hopkins Architects. This mixed use project consists of
a complex of ten buildings creating a network of intimate public spaces.
In contrast to many of the 'mega' commercial projects completed
during the early 2000s, it is intended to be a landmark that is also
human in scale. Hopkins Architects, like many other British practices,
opened an office in the region in the early 2000s, from which it now
works on projects in Turkey, Japan and other parts of the world.

# The new balance of power

As many Western economies went into recession, work in countries such as China, India, Russia and the Middle East became ever more important. Drawing on the example set by American firms, British practices found expansion and agglomeration were key to survival. In 2006, 25% of the world's global architectural firms had British headquarters. By 2011, this figure had held steady, with 24 out of the top 100 calling the UK home.

KK100 Tower, Shenzhen, China, 2004–2011. Farrells. In the 1970s, Shenzhen was a fishing village with a population of 20,000. After being declared as a 'Special Economic Zone' in 1979, the city grew explosively to approximately 8 million people today. This story of growth is matched by many in the region. At 441m high, the tower is the tallest in the world by a British architect. It curves upwards to provide offices, trading floors, an hotel and a panoramic sky garden at its peak.

Interior view of Beijing International Airport, Beijing, China, 2008. Foster + Partners. Conceived on an unprecedented scale and at one point the largest building in the world, the airport was designed and completed in just four years – in time to welcome the world to the 2008 Olympic Games. Its soaring aerodynamic roof is intended to symbolise 'the thrill and poetry of flight', while 'evoking traditional Chinese colours and symbols.'

Masdar Institute, Abu Dhabi, United Arab Emirates, 2010. Foster + Partners. The Masdar Institute was the first part of the wider Masdar city masterplan to be realised and features many design elements encouraging low energy use. With its intimate scale and emphasis on sustainability, the development offers a glimpse of an approach to city-making that may define future development in the region.

British architecture today is an international operation. Of the total income generated by the RIBA's 3,151 registered chartered practices, 20% comes from work outside the UK. For many larger practices the figure is much higher. Designs generated here travel via a network of offices to all corners of the world, taking architecture into new places, at ever greater scales.

As the world has become more interconnected, the distinction of nationality is increasingly unimportant. While in the past 60 years the UK has found fertile ground for its ideas overseas, Britain has continued to be shaped by waves of incoming creative talent and an international outlook that defines its identity.

The UK is the global hub for architecture. Many thousands head here to study and set up practice. London has the world's greatest concentration of architects' practices, engineering and built-environment consultancies. Architecture sits in a fertile melting pot of creative and construction industries, each field pushing the boundaries of the others.

'British architecture' has reinvented itself several times in the post-war years, and is increasingly commissioned, created and owned by a wider community. The Brits may have built much that is striking in the modern world, but it may well be others – trained, influenced and nurtured by them – who build the world we will see tomorrow.

Mike Althorpe, RIBA

# A
# GLOBAL
# ERA

Hugh Pearman

EDITOR, RIBA JOURNAL

# What comes next?

In 2014, the British architectural profession is globally spread as never before. Out of the 27,600 readers of the *RIBA Journal*, for instance, more than 4,400 are based overseas. There are more members of the RIBA in Hong Kong than there are in Wales. There is also a Gulf chapter, while the USA counts as a 'region' with chapters of the Institute in seven places across the continent. To take just one of the game-changing practices covered in this book, Grimshaw's New York office is, in operational terms, now fully two-thirds the scale of its London parent and is the practice's most cosmopolitan venture. 'This is a reflection on New York and in particular the schools of architecture,' remarks Grimshaw deputy chairman Andrew Whalley. 'We have quite large groups from South Korea and China, but also Taiwan, Brazil, Colombia, Mexico and a large contingent from the UK and Australia.' Internationalism pervades the sector in another way: there are increasing numbers of architecture firms which deliberately downplay their point of origin, claim no particular head office and seem to work everywhere.

But any institute can only formalise something once it has happened. Before that comes the exciting and more volatile business of adapting to trade and cultural patterns. In common with other architects working internationally, the British have moved into the BRIC nations – Brazil, Russia, India and China – as well as, increasingly, into the existing and emerging economic powers in Africa and Central Asia. Thus, you find London-based David Adjaye contributing buildings to Moscow, Washington, Oslo and Ghana while a long-established, award-winning multi-regional UK practice, BDP, trades also from Ireland, the Netherlands, the Gulf, India and China.

On a smaller scale, you find a practice such as Edinburgh-based Sutherland Hussey, a well-regarded firm, like most of

Z15 Tower, Beijing, China, 2012–ongoing. Farrells. When completed this tower will be one of the tallest in the Far East.

Heydar Aliyev Center, Baku, Azerbaijan, 2013.
Zaha Hadid Architects.

Overview of the Masdar City Masterplan, Abu Dhabi, United Arab Emirates, 2007–2008. Foster + Partners. This low-rise, high-density development combines state-of-the-art technologies with the principles of traditional Arab settlements to create a desert community that aims to be carbon neutral and zero waste. Orientated around the pedestrian and transit systems, its car free street plan provides shelter from the extremes of the desert climate.

the others mentioned here, with a Stirling Prize nomination to its name, suddenly working simultaneously on a micro and macro scale at opposite ends of the earth. 'At one point,' Charlie Sutherland wrote in October 2013, 'we were planning the eastern expansion of Chengdu in China – with a total population greater than Edinburgh – while our only work in Edinburgh was a 25-square-metre allotment shed that was going through a difficult public consultation.' Now Sutherland Hussey's new City Museum in Chengdu is nearing completion and the experience has led on to other international work. This includes their competition-winning scheme for the former Tempelhof Airport in Berlin, working with Edinburgh colleagues, landscape architects Gross.Max. The old airfield will become a 400-hectare park with new buildings.

Names such as these underpin the better known 'signature architects' from Britain who tend to make the headlines more often – the likes of Zaha Hadid, David Chipperfield, Foster + Partners, Rogers Stirk Harbour + Partners and Wilkinson Eyre with its sleekly eco-tech eye-catching work in Guangzhou and Singapore. And underpinning all this, in turn, is the RIBA-accredited system of architectural education, seen as an international gold standard. The British system is by no means immune from criticism back home, but overseas its emphasis on personal creativity is often seen as a desirable antidote to the more normal business of learning by rote. In other words, there is something about British architectural design vitality that the world wants at all levels. The number of British academics to be found in universities worldwide also testifies to this.

Once again, you could see this as evidence – now well rehearsed through several economic cycles – of how a small country in an economic recession can make a

disproportionately large global impact as its designers follow
the work. The business of trade is one thing, but what about
the altogether trickier business of aesthetics?

Here the 'what next?' question becomes unanswerable,
for now. At the start of this book I mentioned that mid-
1970s moment when one kind of architecture was yielding
to another: a new guard had arrived. Subsequently, we
saw the similar arrival of Post Modernism, the return of
modernism, and the rise of deconstructivism, which led to
the phenomenon of the challengingly shaped 'icon' building.
Not that this was new – in their different ways the older
Pompidou Centre and Sydney Opera House were playing
the icon game, as were St Paul's Cathedral and Stonehenge
– but the phenomenon of the late 20th/early 21st-century
signature building, explored in the latter sections of this book,
was getting close to being a style in itself.

Today, architecture is in a state of complete architectural
plurality. The backlash against the perceived decadence
of the icon era, coupled with economic recession, led to a
'hairshirt' movement in architecture in many areas – i.e.
keep it plain and simple. A new wave of eco-architecture
also came through in the first decade of the 21st century,
from individual houses to complete city districts. 'Energy
Plus' buildings, which can generate more power than they
use, have now started to appear at all scales. Although the
completely energy self-sufficient, waste-recycling skyscraper
(theoretically perfectly possible) has, at the time of writing, yet
to be built. And a new respect has emerged for old buildings,
even relatively recent old buildings. Instead of being seen
as either obsolete and useless, or 'historic' and therefore
precious, they are now regarded more sensibly as a resource,
to be used and, where necessary, adapted.

New Dehli Station, New Delhi, India, 2005 – ongoing. Farrells.
India's rail network has long been the lifeblood of the nation, moving
many millions of people each year. Like other rapidly developing
economies, new rail infrastructure is now viewed as a critical means
to rejuvenate old cities and provide movement for the masses.

But we are all waiting for the next architecture movement. A movement like that seismic shift from old modernism to High Tech, when everything started to change. A Pompidou Centre moment, if you like. I don't know what this equivalently pivotal building will be or where it will be built. Logic suggests that it may well be driven as much by biology as by more conventional 'hard' technology. At times like these, architecture takes on some of the characteristics of religion: we seek the prophet who will show us the way. All I can say is that, given the fertile conditions in which architecture has developed in Britain since the 1950s, we might well start by looking in our own back yard.

Qatar Civil Aviation Authority Headquarters, Doha, Qatar. Grimshaw Architects. Due for completion in 2015.

# Acknowledgements

The RIBA would like to thank the following people and
organisations for their assistance in the production of this book
and the associated exhibitions mounted in 2014.

Mike Althorpe

Catherine Pütz

Hugh Pearman

Charles Hind

Peter Sweasey

Ian McInnes

Robert Adam

Barnabus Calder

Peter Davey

Murray Fraser

James Cubitt & Partners

Foster + Partners

Zaha Hadid Architects

Farrells

Grimshaw

Hopkins Architects

Rogers Stirk Harbour + Partners

Published by RIBA Publishing,
15 Bonhill Street, London EC2P 2EA

ISBN 978 1 85946 527 1

Stock code 81926

The right of the RIBA to be identified as the Author of this Work has been asserted in
accordance with the Copyright, Design and Patents Act 1988.

*British Library Cataloguing in Publications Data*
A catalogue record for this book is available from the British Library.

Publisher: Steven Cross
Designed and typeset by Alex Lazarou
Printed and bound by Butler Tanner & Dennis, Frome and London, UK

While every effort has been made to check the accuracy and quality of the information
given in this publication, neither the Author nor the Publisher accept any responsibility for
the subsequent use of this information, for any errors or omissions that it may contain, or
for any misunderstandings arising from it.

RIBA Publishing is part of RIBA Enterprises Ltd.
www.ribaenterprises.com

# Image credits

Unless stated otherwise, all images: RIBA British Architectural Library Photographs Collection
and RIBA Drawings and Archives Collections.

p 6    Alastair Hunter / RIBA British Architectural Library Photographs Collection
p 8    Daniel Wong
p 9    Duccio Malagamba / RIBA British Architectural Library Photographs Collection
p 11   Farrells
p 12   Nigel Young
p 13   Rick Roxburgh
p 14   Hopkins Architects
p 15   Andrew Zuckerman
p 27   (bottom right) British Airways
p 29   (top and bottom) Henk Snoek / RIBA Photographs Collection
p 31   Hopkins Architects
p 32   (bottom) AP/PA
p 32   (top) British Airways
p 33   (Terry Farrell) Monica Pidgeon / RIBA Photographs Collection
p 33   (Michael Hopkins) Hopkins Architects
p 33   (Patricia Hopkins) Architectural Press Archive / RIBA Photographs Collection
p 34   (bottom) Terry Farrell
p 34   (top) Grimshaw
p 35   Monica Pidgeon / RIBA Photographs Collection
p 36   (top) Rogers Stirk Harbour + Partners
p 37   (top right) Architectural Press Archive / RIBA Photographs Collection
p 37   (bottom left) Originally published in Domus 530, 1974, Casali, Courtesy Editoriale Domus S.p.A., all rights reserved
p 37   (bottom right) John Donat / RIBA British Photographs Collection
p 39   Martin Charles / RIBA Photographs Collection
p 40   (bottom) Rogers Stirk Harbour + Partners
p 40   (top) Emmanuel Thirard / RIBA Photographs Collection
p 41   Foster + Partners
p 42   Foster + Partners
p 43   Alastair Hunter / RIBA Photographs Collection
p 44   (top) Foster + Partners
p 44   (bottom) Jo Reid and John Peck
p 45   (top) Alastair Hunter / RRIBA Photographs Collection
p 45   (bottom) Christopher Hope-Fitch / RIBA Photographs Collection
p 46   (bottom) Lasdun Archive / RIBA Photographs Collection
p 46   (top) Alastair Hunter / RIBA Photographs Collection
p 47   (bottom) Christopher Hope-Fitch / RIBA Photographs Collection
p 47   (top) Ben Johnson
p 49   Cloud 9 Leeds / RIBA Photographs Collection
p 50   (left) UKTI
p 50   (right) Duccio Malagamba / RIBA Photographs Collection
p 51   (left) Iwan Baan
p 51   (right) Richard Davies
p 52   (top) Christopher Hope-Fitch / RIBA Photographs Collection
p 53   (top) Reid & Peck / RIBA Photographs Collection
p 53   (bottom) Heatherwick Studio
p 55   Zhou Ruogu Architecture
p 56   (top) Foster + Partners
p 56   (bottom) Morley Van Sternberg
p 57   (top) Nigel Young
p 57   (top) Christian Richters
p 58   (top) Grimshaw
p 58   (bottom) Helen Binet
p 59   (top) Fosters + Partners
p 59   (bottom left) Monserrat Rubio / RIBA Photographs Collection
p 59   (right) Duccio Malagamba / RIBA Photographs Collection
p 60   (top) BDP
p 61   (left) Eric Firley / RIBA British Photographs Collection
p 61   (right) William Lyons
p 62   John Campbell
p 63   (top) Nigel Young
p 63   (bottom) Nigel Young
p 66   Farrells
p 67   Farid Xayrulin
p 68   Foster + Partners
p 70   Farrells
p 71   Grimshaw